Love | Source | Joy

Mystic Hymns and Sonnets

by

Thomas Bruder

Copyright © 2021 by Thomas Bruder

All rights reserved. No part of this publication may be re-produced, distributed or transmitted in any form or by any means, including photocopying, recording, or other electronic or mechanical methods, without the prior written permission of the publisher, except in the case of brief quotations embodied in critical reviews and certain other non-commercial uses permitted by copyright law. For permission requests, write to the publisher, addressed "Attention: Permissions Coordinator," at the email address below.

Thomas Wang-Bruder
thomas@bruderweb.com
https://thomasbruder.com

Book layout by Kaity Astraelis

Love Source Joy: Mystic Hymns and Sonnets / Thomas Bruder. —1st Ed.

Library of Congress Control Number: 2021917258

Tradepaper ISBN: 978-1-7378-1912-7
Ebook ISBN: 978-1-7378-1910-3

10 9 8 7
1st edition, October 2021

All expressions of love are maximal.

— A Course in Miracles, T-1.I.1.

Dedication

What flower unfurls its lush exuberance,
All verdure, lustrous pink and blushing white?
Nelumbo springing full in warmth and light
Gently above the leaves entangled dense.

Hard-weathered limestone rounds the water line;
Shaded, the pointy-roofed pavilion rooms;
In zigzag patterns past the fragrant blooms
Unfold by footpath: bamboo, plum and pine.

Yielding, the surface stirs as sheen and breeze
Upward mirror each image passing by;
Aroma, tranquil flows, reflected sky
Now deepen, blend their rich profundities.

Introduction

The pieces set forth in this little volume are exercises in word music; music that would flow unaccompanied by instrumentation, and, perhaps, with no sound at all; words that would transmit a fullness of experience, with phenomena, thought and mood unified and immediate.

The Sonnets to the Aten are the earlier compositions, the form, with its rigidity and compression, being ideal for the development of style. Mystic Hymns and Psalms presents a freer hand, more attuned to fluidity, spontaneity, the living; life itself. The Asterism Sonnets, written last, aim to replicate certain features of the ghazal.

The author draws heavily from the Hymn to the Aten, Psalm 104 (especially the translation by Robert Alter), the music of Sun Ra, and other sources. And from the indomitable, the cultivated in its roughness, the wildly curated, the blessed spirit of the Arlington Garden in Pasadena, surely the grace and future of this Earth.

T.W-B.
Los Angeles, June 29, 2021

A. Mystic Hymns and Psalms

1.

Blinds raised, unlatched, our open windows let
Wavelets of softest luminescence in;
Fresh clarities expand in these crisp chambers
Painting as if each inch in light were painted,
And gushed perfume of candied roses comes,
Up-currents, nostril gladdening, sweet scents
To swoon and waken us too long with labors
Held down, quite down; outside, orange-crested birds
Of paradise, sway-faced, give quizzical
Sharp looks, turn random-wise in puzzlement
As engines sputter by; and all is freshness,
Renewal, spring in winter, burgeon, sap;
This day, dear heart, we let us this day open
The cluttered inward; let reverberation
Of endless source, source endless, welcome us.

2.

Rolling inward, the pewter clouds prevailed
Grey skies to greyer darknesses returning,
When sudden brilliance, flaring, dazzled straight,
Beaming photonic flows to ray the nimbus,
Converging fresher mists and warmer sheens;
My crumpled car by crumbling blocks I parked
Walking along decrepit masonries,
As upward yearned the shaggy-bearded palm trees;
Motor exhaust and pine in breezes breathing
By charming shops that resin incense waft,
Dear friend of shared antiquity I met,
With smoky teas and plated, earthen foods
Of rooted succulence, as heightened spirits
Our airs encircled, words to startle ears
At neighbor tables uttered; brother, now
Shaking the antique dust from these old shoulders,
We join the endlessly renewed renewal.

3.

Source, joy; once joined the coil and bulb, the charge
That through us constant incandescence sheds;
Lantern, no matter how ornately shaped,
Inert and cold, when raised, the fiery wick
That makes the chambered brightness beacon outward;
Or twiggy torch, the ember-glow that flames
And burning bends the dark against the night;
But if, my heart, you'd greater valence have,
Nothing outbests to be no thing at all,
And nothing better than this formlessness
Where image fixed may no more fixate thinking;
—Illness-injured, I lay there, madly fevered
As day and night were blurred, a bed of twisted
Shivers, the winter coat beneath thick blankets,
Layered, couldn't give comfort; throaty wounds,
Infection's focus, salted, scalding, screamed,
Bayed in a mouth of blisters moaning; frailer
The limbs, the corpus frail, as failed the ricey
Porridge obstructed swallowings to pass,
But, lungs inflamed, dry bellows blasted, hacked
And hacked, I coughed, my corpse contorted, bent
As cold hands pressed the keys along the spine,
And pile of pills to raise this febrile lich
Deep wooziness induced, then day to night
Night day replaced; but now, I, artless, see
The dawning air is crisply circling garment
Of dazzles spread against the springing world;
Now, rugged firs of hirsute emerald stand
Fresh among branches winter-stripped, bone-fingered,
And healing rays that nourish, captured, flash
In the palm fronds, redden the umber walls

And ocher bake of burnt and rounded stone,
The zigzag paths of garden beds, where sweetly
The swaying honeysuckle drips; those paths
I'll walk again, together, where, we joining,
We're not the things we seem to be, but limit
Leaving, we'll know our joy is source; source, joy.

4.

Maze within maze that spins the outer spirals
Through dusty circuits; bends the inner ramps
Pillared, lapping, overlapping; that lifts
Shelter to break the sky's hot blazes; ranker
Trash at the feet of close tent-sleepers heaps,
Where lively draw the eye the painted murals;
Bumper to bumper whirls like winds or slow
Slower, stopping, like dung by beetles, rolls;
Partitions bluntly concretized, that passes;
Tangles of roadway thicket, prickly pear
Inmixed, high-stalked agave lining clumps
Of earthy hillets, loops; where shimmer towers
That upward loom pristine in order, hastens,
We drive, until more splendid streets we see,
Parking though signs forbid the non-permitted,
To watch on heaven's lawns the gentlest rays
Touching the lemon buds, the fuchsia climber
That burstful juts; our city's jumbled parts
Will find us no ways lost when everything
That is or seems is dearest, deepest joy.

5.

Even now, mid-February, though unblossomed
The wildflower fields like twisted thicket lie
And lowly crust the rustling ground the leaves,
Bees at the torchy aloe's clusters buzz:
As warm rays nourish, look, they droning land,
Minute rapidities in rich abundance,
Fervent for scarlet saggings, nectar ooze;
Now come, my heart, where dangled voltage lines
Droop from the splintered poles that lean, and gleam
Old shops of clashing hues, angles refreshed,
Fronting the curvy roads that weather, cracked,
With oil, exhaust and decades' dust begritted;
Now fanning palms their desiccated fronds
Our welcome wave from hills that undulate
Dry, scrubby brush to distant, purplish hazes;
And stony cliffs now mark our path, that, spilt,
Prismatic pigments flowing rainbow-bannered;
Nearby, at makeshift canopies we'll have
Lavendered, honeyed coffees ground and poured,
Where plank the tables potted succulents,
And bamboo rods the twirling vines up-creep
Along the turquoise masonry; bent bars
On windows bolted guard the artist's shop
Whose doors are open, look, and now, heart, have:
This rich bouquet's most fragile peonies
All verdures, blushing creams and creamy blush,
Swooning, my love, whose lovely these exceeds,
And, marry me, and, happy birthday, sweetest.

6.

Leisurely stroll past canvas canopies,
The air enriched by garden sprigs new-plucked,
Where shady tables show the earth's rich bounties,
Diversely vested persons; as squat urns,
Clumped succulents whose fractal-patterned shoots
Shoot strangely higher, painted curbs adorn;
And walls flanking the concrete walkways sheen
Aquatic scenes of goldfish gilded, blues
More vivid flowingly emmuraled; puffing
Of pungent incense by the breezes drifts,
Teases the nostrils; waiting, waiting, I
Beside the little, stained-glass rose mosaic
Watch as the hilly splendors downward stretch
The morning shadows; watch my watchful love
Who, lovely, closer, closer joining comes.

7.

Along the roadway's cyclic rage, cement
And parching dirt with tangled weeds up-slope;
In trash, discarded shards and fencing bent
Spring lucid poppies, orange, vermilion-bright
Petals like flame, like silken, dawning light.

8.

Silence will I, my heart, heart's cantor, hate,
The ringing quiet that wrings clamorless,
Or dread the brimful cup's full emptiness
As gritty drops that nourished dissipate?

Lament that lovely things we cultivate
In vacancy, now wilting, evanesce;
That frenzied works, no matter mad excess,
Still end in stillness, mutely terminate?

But no; in silence hymns all source all being;
The blooming void reveals itself prolific
And fertile flourishes its seeming bareness.

Senseless, the manic flight to sensuous fleeing
When stillness shows all things as beatific;
The verse is not the words but this awareness.

9.

City at evening's light sprawl spiraled glows
In phantom patterns, nighttime punctuates,
Beacons with mazy orbs the dimmer streets
That viewless sink to inky nothingness;
The wider roads continue blankly, seldom
Does other driver our slow drive deflect
But car, unhurried, fluent moves, when now
The rushing hour would rampant traffic halt;
And though the buildings glimmer, neon-lined,
Strange apparitions in the distance looming
And oddly lucent, I know no one's there
By stately order; precious person bearing,
Cross we the crumbling vastness, port approaching,
That voided still its sheened array displays,
Unpeopled, save the central terminal;
Passengers drop, garages vacant, park,
Where echoes space that empty spaces fill,
And exit, prophylactic mask and gloves
Tightened, the touch of walkway button shunning;
Then sliding doors reveal them, hundreds hushed:
They stand in rows divided, sterile suits,
Protective gear and hazard mask secured,
Figures along the looping segments linked,
The luggage stacked that strain to grip or push,
Each one contagion to the other, crowded,
They zigzag inching toward the counters, murmur
The only noise, or infant crying, carriage
Shielded with plastic sheets, while overhead
Speakers the massive chambers shrilly charge,
Directing each their final flights abroad,
Until each, guarded, gateward filing steps,

And there our loved one goes, alone, she waving,
Ascending, waves, alone, she disappearing;
Later returned, I, clothes discarded, bathe,
And sleeping, dream; asleep, I, dreaming, see
In darker waters, deeper darknesses
And violent upsurge surge Leviathan,
Whose gaping maw is than all bodies greater.

10.

This cramped apartment, unit crammed apart
That narrow seems and daily narrower,
Strictly defines our worry, work, and world
As day to night, night day us daze, restricted
Realm of our anguished lockdown, living pent;
Pajama-bodied, tousled hair, distracted,
Find I myself at table, couch or chair
Chair, table, couch to while the idle hours
Watching the rainy street where trafficless
Dim figures masked themselves pass distancing
As drizzle drips down limpid glass and leaf;
And yet this day while awkward calisthenics,
Blinds closed, I underclothed again begin,
Most rote routine to render limber limbs,
Flash of an image struck me starting startled,
The inner sight more real than outer seeming;
Great silhouette I saw beneath great rays
On grassy cliffs that seaward face, where path
Pebbled along the outcrop slopes; of shimmers
The shadow, featureless, but sun-bejeweled
Its brilliant crown of dazzles, purest light
That emanates, corona shedding, spheres
Of wavy luminescence, constant waves;
Then, spread across the earth, its like I saw,
One from one thousand, two, ten thousand, joined
As darling rays the darker globe encompassed;
Most holy of our kind, you wholly kindly,
Teach us to heal this day this mind, us healing,
That we may think with you and be one mind.

11.

The Pleiades while Venus lovely passes,
Our distant cousins closer greetings giving,
Making of magnitudes a silvery torch
To grace the faded city's blocked horizon,
Freed from our daily cells, our nightly walks
We take beneath the outstretched voltage lines
And orb-topped columns faintly glowing; night
Its vanishings in all things stitches, shape
And tint with wispy evanescence shrouding;
The fragrant rose bush sticking from the fence,
Its folded blooms full bursting, hides its hues
In scented dwindlings, walking we beside,
And knitted canopies of trees now blot
The starry heavens, starry heavens bare
Again, as, fresh, the air is richly swirling,
With jasmine, eucalyptus, honeysuckle
Laden, the breezes sweetly flowing; look,
Red bottlebrush in up-cast beams is beaconed,
And there pink trumpets' colors ghostly show
Tender about the greyish trunk, and there
Blood oranges plumply dangle from the limbs
That leafy rest on iron gratings, gathered,
Their charms, in artificial lambencies;
No car the roadway maddens, and no other
Specter appears in murky background stepping,
But silence holds, or distant motor droning;
Now heavy ploddings upward lead us where
Angular mansions mount the hilly levels,
In which, exquisite homes, none live, it seems,
Though sloping driveways wind; not far from here,
Not far, our brothers in adjoining tents,

Together pitched apart, they sleeping lie
Or under lamps that buzz they, blanketed,
The naked back against the pavement, watch
Slow orbit of that tidal ship that sends
The radiance that to earth rebounded bounds;
To elements, dear brothers, we exposed,
As moonlight I'm become, remotely viewing:
May I be fit to bathe your blessed feet.

12.

Expanse of stars against the endless pitch
I watch, a vivid dream or traveling
By subtle, astral art, not knowing which,
But freely go as visions swooping swing;
A grand hotel along the moon-sparked sea
Remote to me my lucid viewings bring,
And earthward arcing, plunging rapidly
Within a cellar near the kitchen find
My ghost amid stored foods, utensilry;
There huddle other figures there confined,
The persons neither clear nor clearly penned,
I pensive float beside as formless mind,
Awaiting what they anxiously attend;
Not long, when opening the cellar door,
Unearthly entities the steps descend;
More detail would I give, but detailed more
Dim memory remembering prevents;
Outside, we darkling walk the starry shore,
While cunning use of psychic implements
Renders the craft a car of subtle sheen
And stranger garb as human suits presents
That peering eyes may see us, nothing seen;
A parking lot we cross, where bluish flashes,
As each now boards, the circular machine.
Before my spirit back to body crashes
To don again its clunky, earthen gear,
Prime vehicle that sense to itself lashes,
I watch the upward rising vessel veer
Swiftly above the palms and pampas grass;
It blinks, then joins the outer atmosphere.
You visitors that mark this humble mass

And tread its surface, what maneuvers tempt?
What business have you as you planet pass,
In orbit of our love drawn, non-exempt.

13.

Warmer the sun compacted pathway heats
Of dirt and rounded stony edging; flowing
The breeze befruited stem and stalkling meets
As lizards scamper, belly burning; throwing

Shadows the droopy pepper branches; sways
Matilija tall-bloomed its eggy petals
Wrinkled; sweetly the smoky fragrance plays
Of purple sage with incense of dry nettles

Blown, with the bees so fully inward steeped
You scarcely hear their buzzing; dizzy math
Aeonium folds outward, foldings heaped,
Plastic perfections multiplied, as path

Returning turns where swiftly darting bicker
The hummingbirds that hover, lovely elves,
Chilopsis lapping; dangle quickly quicker
Barberry sprigs, and prickly pear themselves

Selves upward send; the clumpy milkweed pod
And buckwheat bend by plump, serrated aloe;
My love, we find us in love's temple, odd
Among the spikes of orangish desert mallow.

14.

Aeonium, your proper I've not done
Praises; your black rose charms me more than any
Rose, and your burly stem turns, little sun,
Its dark rays bursting, manifold and many

Folded; each plushy leaflet, spiking, beams
Like day on glossy beetles striking; musing
Is mind subsumed along your spirals, dreams
Of chitin, clover, pomegranate fusing

Rosettes like supple lions' manes; my yearning
Your cultivars has cultivated; thought
Has thought to count your panicles, discerning
The flare of yellow pyramidions; caught,

I sense concentric patterns pointing toward
Infinities; though unlike those of roses,
Your scentless petals fume the void, adored
I've often your enigmas over nose's

Reward; your blades' plasticities and poses
Give sharper shape to twisted desert flora,
As looming you the dirt beshadow; closes
My ode your maker praising: heightened aura

Of island genius, engineering, linked
You, set you forth adorning, madly brained,
The tech that brought them to the brink extinct;
Collapsed the culture, aeons you remained.

15.

Drizzly with droplets air suffused we breathing,
And holding hands, meander languid, watching
Our world that greyish gives phenomena
Of cooler June, its misty glooms, its breezes
That rainless rush the tangled plots, the weedy
And jolted pavement slabs beside which bounce
Sheeny and sleek the crows picking the grasses,
Grim harbingers I know not whether; cars
Now whizzing whir and whirring whiz us past
They going where? But we abundant gardens
To see will take us nearer, neighborhood
Of rented units lively, livelier made
With public access; cactus and orange groves
Greenly entrance the gravel road, but we'll
Where myrtle, sweetly understated, sighs
With richer scents along the path's allée
Aligned, the finely stamened petals open,
Footing the pebbles go; like colonnades
The twisted olive trees the courtyard gracing
With silver-green the leaves oblong, and furry
The textured cypress twirlers twirling higher
Than droop of cables; other persons masked
We masking pass, our muffled hellos heard;
And gourdy cheeks most charming deeper swell
Of pomegranate budding ruddy, trickling
The dewy branch its condensation; wishing
Trees that display their hand-marked gallery,
Notations scrawled of intimate-most yearnings,
Dangling, their messages transmit; but troubled
We stand in paradisiac settings, brooding,
Eyes closed, boots and batons and toxic gases

Seeing, a phalanx armed that armored crushes
A screaming populace, the streets in wreckage,
As horror, captain, takes the city captive,
The mind imprinted has; but glimpse the eyes
Against the vaporous fabric of the forest
Leaflets and florets, ruptured artichoke,
Its dreamy purple blossom brightly now,
Although the stalk be trampled, blooming is,
Obliquely bent against the beaten soil;
Who stepped on you, my dear, you dearly vivid,
Magnificence by what, on what ground trodden?
The flower by multilayered heart sustained,
A spirit moves among us merging now
Fields of expansive love, your loveliness.

16.

Passing Edenic realms we streets reenter
Where strangely city's latent energies
Are, most erratic flowings, manifest;
Mismatching roads, dismantled, motors veer
Now all, now none, now faster, slower pressing
With sudden lane, change sudden, unforeseen,
My dear, my steady pilot, piloting,
And watch we now opaquely levitate
Skyscrapers in the heated wispiness
Of haze and scorchy elements that weather
The lumbrous poles that age has pulled, the speary
Lamps from their irons scratching airy billows;
And stone of stores decrepit, boarded, chained
By which with none on board the buses run
Fresh galleries of sprayed graffiti spanning
Livelier, bolder show; blinding the sun,
The roadways sinuous, the curvy driftings,
Pedestrians each from each other distanced,
Not congregating, sparsely walk; and where
Construction once was busy builded, still
And silent rise the cranes, the scaffolding,
Flimsy retaining walls and empty floors;
The longer tunnel now we turning enter
Trash and debris scattered and strewn and tents
Along the dayless dimness wading; pigeons
Themselves on dusty concrete, bathing, sun
With twitch of wings beside the chain link fences
At tunnel's end; where highway intersects
Degraded overpass, erupts the sudden,
The spriggy palo verde trees that spread
With podded foliage fiery yellows breathing

All day of cars the harsh exhaust; but how
My dear, too long that we've not seen them, how
Can we our loved ones visit, past the murals,
The fanning palms, the sharply painted shops,
When simple gathering can poison, so
We're told, and we our little one, our blessed
Secret, must now protect, this day of June,
Two thousand twenty, twenty-seventh, driving.

17.

Unrolled along the floor's taut rug a mat,
The planky hardness softened just enough,
I have, my back against it flatly pressed,
My heels against the lower portion pushed,
And towel for blanket, too, becomes ideal,
While agitated body calm would be
Before to bed returning; sleepless flung,
Old clothes as worn pajamas, fidgeting,
As swelter of the day recedes, and cooler
The evening settles; whirs the droning filter
Faintly beside me, subtle glow suffusing
On shady walls and darker furnishings,
Umbra, penumbra casting; twisted blinds
The beams of motors gunning by diffuse,
Glancing along the room they glide; outside
Along the south horizon flicker drifting
Jupiter, cheery torch, ash-ember Saturn,
Suspended where the glare the emptiness
Touches, toward Sagittarius dimly marked,
And there Antares ruddy shimmers; hours
I lie as heart against the ribcage heaves
And restlessness the limbs inhabits, shifting
My presence, comfortable, uncomfortable,
While wander, absent, mind's imaginings;
Such things I see demolishing all sleep,
As loss of loved ones, penury, affliction,
The food bank lines, the viral testing lines,
Of them who stand the midday heat, I think,
Each ordered six, each from each other, feet;
Though phantom we, I love you, phantoms each,
And now impediment this love can't pass

There's none; against the lidded eye I see,
As clearly as against the screeny ceiling,
Patterns of lighted shapes that flowing stream,
As mind's geometer the darkness measures,
Endless with spirals spiral-springing, rapid
Forms within forms, returning, turning, turns
The mind the void it circles, the, the, the;—
Unrolled along the floor's taut rug a mat...

18.

Now magnified the heat the pavement bakes,
And gold medallions circle now the trees
With coils of bold bouquets the ferny leaflets;
The slightest walking sweat induces now,
And skimpy fabric closer clinging grips,
Each step an effort, blinding overhead
The candors, as we each our shelter masked
To breathe the fresher air would flee; so many
Crowding the streets, so many each avoidant,
As if each symptomless the virus sheds,
And death invisible; resound the blocks
Where parrots, red-crowned, ululating perch
And greenly gliding cast their feral shrieks,
Echoed hysterics; red the spanning wings,
The speculum with feather flourish showing;
And crisper now the brush is rendered; stirring,
Each startled thing that scurries flimsiness
Crinkles, and all for water calls, all dust;
Though verdures of grey-mottled sycamores
Now browning shrivel on the branch and droop,
Lushness enough the pathway shady keeps;
Seated, we watch the butterflies that flit
Along the breeze, that flutter kindly past
Our bench, secluded, where, most criminal,
As thieves that moments of great moment take,
We drop our masks, we breathe each other's air;
And now in naked beams that burn the soil
We pass where just last week the artichoke
I saw, my dear; its purple tufted glory,
Is clipped and gone, the rooty husk dried out,
And absent air remains; this world is not

Our home, our feet don't flatly stride or stand
On firm earth firmly, but we loving topple;
And though our little one we'll soon deliver,
We'll teach her too what means it human being
To be, and not to be, but merely love.

19.

Thrownness

At first, in sense-phenomena we find
Ourselves unquestioning but we accept
The meanings to the senses mind assigned
Bundled together but unconscious kept;
So thrown, we seem to live what mind designed
In seamless order while the mind has slept,
And sleeping strive to keep the self employed
To seek its comfort, harsher things avoid.

Time

Our memory our story seems to tell
And we to it with clutching fingers cling;
The past is gone but we assume it well
Coheres to tell us what today will bring;
But mind imposes this self-weaving spell;
The past is present wish and picturing;
The now is not a time the senses sense;
Reviewing past we view as present tense.

Dread

And this ensures the future's like the past;
Between the two a madness from within
Erupts with shiverings that body blast,
And chilly currents prick the tingled skin;
We horrid seem, more horrid we don't last
Or wishing we might end or not begin;
Until our dread a prison is that we,
Confining us, can't think to break or flee.

Mind

Illusions though don't brandish true effects;
Two thoughts I have, I have both unaware;
The one the world of penury projects;
The other phantom sees and empty air;
I view all horrors as the mind directs
While kindly stillness dazzles everywhere;
One thought undoes the world the other makes;
And thinker thinking loveliness now wakes.

Awakening

The water lily that lay hidden grows,
In dusty nothing live and lush it springs,
Where easeful now the fertile river flows
A constant source that nourishes all things;
The Aten, inward shining, outward glows,
Embraces all and gentle warmness brings,
And find we now our home as present we
Join all creation, joyful endlessly.

20.

Deep night, when one eye can't another see
Or barely sees, as strapped the mask our breathing
Rebounding fogs our glasses; tottering,
Blindly we cross the curb, we awkward stumble
The walkway down, beneath, weirdly, the buzzes
Of saffron sending lamps, electric hues
At points arranged, making the boughs look burning,
Whose conic radiations downward show
Us twin ghosts ambling, apparitions strange,
Appearing, disappearing, night again;
And road beside us lengthens ever, few
Signals to stop the traffic rise, but race
The cars with echo of mad engines driven,
Then darkly vacant all; invisible
Chirp strident crickets creaking, screech the bats
That clumsy flutter chittering among
The waxy-leafed magnolia trees; and trots
Silence itself the lawn along with bushy
Tail and with up-perked ears, it listens, sharply
Pointed, indifferent to our faster passage,
Crouching coyote; filaments that brush
Now arms, now legs and faces, trailing threads
That drift along the breezes, sudden clingings
The spiders leave, we breaking scrape us free;
And, pendent jewels, the sky's exquisite fires,
They twinkle diamond, ruby faceted,
The bar, the tail of Scorpio expansive,
Curving along the massive fabric, haze
Of city interference, depths of space,
With ruddy ardors smoldering and lit.
Ambulate motors that bipedal heave

The human frame, us homeward now convey;
The night is deep and I my wearied being
To sleeplessness would lay me and commend;
Bless oh my being my Being, all source, all life,
Infinity extending, wholly joyous
And ceaselessly creative; my frail puppet
Foregoing, absence gone, I present am:
And I would know You dreaming and awake.

21.

Bless oh my being my Being, all source, all life,
Infinity extending, wholly joyous
And ceaselessly creative, Who now dawns
Lovely in light fields, shimmer-garmented,
With dazzling rays that rosy wash the buildings,
That warm the granite, piercing flash-reflected
The glass, the mirrors crystalline; they flow,
Vast waters nourishing all things, the beams
You emanate, sky-flooding waves that would
All peoples gladden, comforting; Who blinks
Traversing earth than thought-speed faster, here,
Now there at will, as clouds You glancing gather,
Disperse, all planes and times Your vessels crossing,
Dimensions, all; Who brightens everywhere;
Jumbled the mix of bristly hills, the structures,
The desert valleys richly planted, roads
That ramp on columns, multi-graded, rising
At curvy junctions, strain decayed as stream
All traffic lanes, all start and stop in You,
The crafted metals flare Your rapid splendors;
I, early rising, city wander squinting,
With little sleep, my evening troubles weighing,
But drowsily to work rote labors go,
And do not see; if I my drab awareness
Could swiftly shift, the body, heart-elated,
I'd leap, all soul in jubilee I'd lift;
The mazy passages the heaps of trash
More densely piling line and pigeons pick
Beneath, of scraggly palms, the dwindling ribbons
That wither trailing from the trunks, they soak
Your sustenance, pristinely gleaming, all,

Though harsh the sun that burning dries them, drawn
Midway along its fiery circuit, winds
That parch the heated surface sending; sprigs
From pavement cracks in-rooted Who entices
To spring and leaves unfurl and budding bloom
Suffusing color through the tender petals,
Resolving all potentials toward Your warmth,
Your boundless love; our daughter yet unborn
Who knows, in Whom reclining, swaddled softly,
She thinks You and is thought by You, and we,
Her parents, too; the oceans teeming leap
Alive with You, the briny surf that breaking
Pummels the shores, Whose droplets, tidal spray
Wind-glistening, the face now freshen, glimmer
Now magnify, as ships Your liquid canvas
Engine across; the dolphins mind-connected,
That sleekly skim the undulance and beam
Among them agile knowings, easeful move
In Your placidities; the blue whales boldly
Up-submarine from darker depths to glide
The waters parting, tail the foamy wake
Behind them turning, all astonished leave,
All self I'd lose in Your grand magnitudes;
My mind to Your vast channels, may it be
Ever attuned, Your rays, while eye I use
To see will see and voice to name will name,
You ever-center of my always thoughts,
Until we joining disappear within You,
Formless, expansive, endless, knowing: One.

22.

Hotly the earth the heavens scorch, and dryly
Late summer vegetation brittle renders,
The lively moisture lost, the shriveled shape
Leaving; suspended particles the air
Now heavy settle, tawny tinging, sickly,
A haze of vast incinerations raging
The countryside across, the ashen fallout
Falling, all breath with brim inhaled, as rubble,
Debris and ruin place replace; how long
Humanity its holding holds, the planet
Poisoned? The engines that our commerce drive,
Consumptive, few enriching greatly, many
Poorly in penury, how long combusting
The soil itself can we continue? Surely
Last night a strange, foreboding omen ruddied
The sky, when Mars, the bloody glimmer, grew
Hornlike the cratered surface over, Moon
Conjoining, reddish pallors jointly casting,
Ensorcelled emanations, meaning what
I do not know; but morning come, our world
Awoke infernal glowings witnessing,
As hellish fires the landscape now devour
And flooding, hurricane, tsunami, drought
Elsewhere the globe to cataclysm hasten;
Our wish to see a new Atlantis rising,
Most intricate with nature integrated,
A greener earth, free energies all peoples
Freely flowing our grasp is slipping, leaping
From view; content to bless this world, all things
Releasing, grieved, forgiving, injured, healing,
Each person wholly worthy seeing, I
Must be, when rage would further damage wreak.

23.

Maybe three days, four days, I've not my unit
Left, but the trash accumulating, bagged
In plastic drawn I'll to the dumpster take,
Releasing me from lockdown momently
To breathe the evening air, but agitated,
Circles encircles, spotlight beaming, beating
The chill with heavy blades, the helicopter,
Its engine madly frantic, goes, the manic
Rotations alleys echo mechanized,
Throughout reverberating; garbage hoisted
Crashes with clink of glass on metal, lid
Resounding shuts, it slams despite my effort,
Who tranquil nighttime denizen would be,
And still it circles searching; rivulets
The sprinkler system hissing pools and puddles,
The gutter rushing, automated trickles
With angry twirlings, lifted from dry lawns,
And semaphores now red, now green, now red
Again now signal, traffic stopping, starting,
As rapid motors, cyclic, growl and gun
Or idle bide the sequent color switches,
And pilot now controlled careenings leaves
Departing, gone; the gap a stillness fills,
The half-moon horns curve upward, Jupiter
Beneath, that dazzling shows, and Saturn dimmer,
They downward stream their steady luminescence,
And Mars the eastward, orangely glowing ember
So closely floats, that distant eons back
Was oceanic, fertile, sustenant,
It seems as though its surface I might touch
Mere thought extending; has my time shut in

Made eye so sensitive the glimpse of things,
Disturbing, fascinates? This world repeats,
Repeats its cycles heedlessly recycled,
Machinely piloted without me; me,
Indoors I'll keep, my keyboard hunching over,
The bluish screen that flickers vision seizing,
Meeting my work demands as if this world
Were not calamitous; but dreaming peace.

24.

Will I allow myself indulgence this,
That I the body of a loved one mourn,
Strong arms that carried infant me I miss,
And raised me to adulthood to him born;
I know we're not our bodies, know that death
Does not us end but ending separates
The mind its manikin and pseudonym,
And yet as body heaves its final breath,
Though I remember lives and prior fates,
Composure crumbles, and loss operates
To strike me dumb, I merely mourning him.

The virus us from visiting has kept
Who many lands and peoples many passed
In happy times, but plague does not except
Us mourners, as we shelter, stationed fast.
Though there I cannot be, my brother, there
My thoughts to you are instant beams directed
Thinking the many kindnesses that I
Would tender sicker body, sharper care;
I'd tell us this the world that we've projected
And, though the image dwindles, we connected
Forever are where minds don't lives belie.

This world a simulation is and seems
True place that we inhabit as true ghosts
Eking existence while our willful dreams
Would make of captive minds unknowing hosts;
It seems that us infirmity and age
Pursuing shed all earthly gains in losings,
And comforts won our comfort render never;

But wise among us face illusions sage,
Not victim to the idle world's abusings;
Accept, my father, these my frantic musings:
I miss you now and love you now and ever.

25.

Outside, just past the glassy panels (where,
As simulacra of the changing season,
The hybrid saucers pinkish, purple sprang,
And lushly green, and brownly crumpled dry
From arid sizzlings, agitated their
Detrital stem and branch extended shift),
Autumnal breezes cooler flowing, bluish,
Greyish the dawn, the dwindling light appear,
As summer's yellows, oranges dissipate,
And still in lockdown sit we cloistered, seldom
Our cells we leave unless necessities
We needing gather, nestled pregnantly,
Awaiting happy times to meet again;
How long since last communal cooking we
Enjoyed? Since fragrant wine was open, aired
And freely poured, with berry, tannin, rot
The glassware ruby turning; pans and burners
Swelter as chef to music through the speakers
Blasted bounces; the table set, the plates
With many chairs and cheer and laughter had,
How long? And now our backs are bent in grief;
Your letter, that you left me, words like stars
That light the dark, like diamonds set, they shine
And twinkling seem, forever will I keep,
And see you too when comes the other time;
Though sorrow brightly through me burning now,
My ego's effigy collapsing, singes
To cinders, yet the body's death does not
Us separate; but death's true meaning yields
This truth: we always insubstantial were
That moved about these phantom planes, like life

At best, at worst, like death, but now, my father,
We know where gleams the living, life itself,
And, lively, see you, love you, everywhere.

26.

With pumpkin now apartments, houses are
Displayed, and other, artificial gear
Of cobweb, wolf and cat, and avatar
The driveway haunting, dimly lit, and near

The massive fig whose curvy roots the soil
With elephantine tendrils looping spread,
As lamp prodigious trunk, the python coil,
And canopy of figments overhead,

That octopus of trees, illumines; moon
In fullness demi-parted clouds disclose,
The moonray muted, seen, but drifting soon
The clouds recover darkly; shadow goes,

My lonesome image, walking road and hill;
I see the courthouse tower that dignifies,
Bold ornament, the mists, and step until
I hear the echo rumbling ground to skies,

The thousand angry engines, unison
Of grumblings, faint reverberation first,
Then louder growling, cylinders that gun,
As if hell open, earthly quaking, burst,

And troop of phantom motorcycles gave;
I stop to watch the riders, steady stream
Of spectral figures riding frames that they've
With eerie neon, flame and chromy gleam

Ghostly assembled, driving strident by,
No sooner manifest, that fuming leave,
The din of motors fading; homeward I
Now take me, witness, this all hallows' eve.

27.

My fear, pervasive, hovers, viewless god
That more than body shakes my inner keeping;
I'd show me normal, if I may, but odd
I feel myself, my heart its rhythm leaping;
How many minutes, hours have dizzy I
With awkward step and flimsy, shuffling gait
Around my dark apartment lapping passed?
Or strewn among the cushions might I lie
Waiting for body to release the weight
As numbness, slow, my person tethers fast?

Coherent consciousness no longer flows,
And thing I thought my thinking occupied
A second past is whisked away as those
Divided moments moment subdivide;
Confused, I cannot fumbling do the math,
The package held, the blurry figures reading,
How far beyond the dose I've overdosed,
But guess the droplets make me psychopath
Who remedy for sleep ingested needing
And suffer thus, a sad, tormented ghost.

Now harder, faster beats my heart, I watch
If further toward unconsciousness I tending
Existence in and out would blinking botch
Not just my sleep but hasten harsher ending.
I do not know the thing I am, or where
Or how to find myself the firmer ground,
But standing seem a shapeless fog to float;
As, legs not walking, hands not holding, air,
My fumbling fingers lemon, water found,
A cup to soothe my cottonmouth and throat.

Again I, downward drifting, awkward fall,

As cheek against the couch is heavy pressed,
A spinning room, faint lamp and shadows all,
In which I'd fitful sleep and panic rest;
My folded self, the trashcan at my side,
You must, my dear, have waking kindly seen
And blanket draped on limbs that shiver bare;
Forgive your foolish husband, who has tried
To render easy, easeful sleep serene
But eyed instead the furies pacing there.

They say that fear is fabric of all dreams,
But love the thread to waking leads; I know
It's true, and know I squander life in seems
So long as through this world I fearful go;
The windows now the dawn-suffusing skies
Reveal, and day its labor gathers speeding;
Content I am to lie here, weary heap,
And, passive, shutter body's active eyes;
The madness of my troubled night receding,
We gently waking give us gentle sleep.

28.

Again, the grid vacated is, the same
Curtains of glassy steel, metallic, lithic
Encasings samely glint and glitter, foil
The solar gust the alleys streaking, hurling
Blindly the dusky umbrage faceted,
As faces warp and ripple, lengthening,
But none to walk the streets appear except
Some blocks away the medic vehicles
Urgently strobing; still the pyramidion
Presides the cypress dry, the fountains drained
Over, the gardens ever green, the turf
Its artifice not real; goodbyes I give,
Who'll seated not again in this perch labor;
And as the midday twilight pales, we see
Along the many lanes the flames erupting
Of maple, fraxinus and sweetgum, reds
And scorchy yellows fanning, sycamores
That crisp and crumpled dump detritus down,
Darker, richer the soil, the fresher mess;
And yet with vigor life in winter thrives:
While palmer's plated armory enfolds
Its folded self with hunkering rosettes,
The foxtail brandishes its loopy stalk
Of budded jade, and strange asparagus
The centuries with nectar splayed display,
Tubular vials high, higher; charming pends
The orange's globe among the petty groves,
Whose leafy surging verdance eye enchants
Against, amorphous dead, the thicket tangles;
This holy day, one year since last we said:
"The slats untwist, the windows we unlatch;"

I think me now the gates of hell did open
Releasing us; now foot the soggy ground
Impresses, gate of horn transparent passes;
Leaving the shades, I dearest carry with me
My adorations, bosom biding, gladly;
Unearthly glow, expansive, airy spanning
The forestry, that plays and playful dances
The breeze along, that leaflet moves and limb,
Now warmly summons this my ghostly rising
Spirit to join its gentlest subtleties;
And I would find what lights the silhouettes.

29.

Amazingly the freeway moving, we
The rushing veer of swoopy vehicles
Avoid, but slowly glide the slower lanes,
The massive trucks behind, our modest car
The faded paint and rapid signs pursuing
Of uncongested interchange; the sky,
Its greyness brindled dark or tawny, rolls,
Hoisting a multi-layered canvas that
The naked, beam diffusing eye deflects;
And road, uneven, slabby concrete ribbed,
That rubber tread of swervy tires has marked,
Smudging the fissured shabbiness, the frame
And steering vibrate driving over; there
Beyond the cinder walls cemented, hills
Dotted with shrubby dirt, or, igneous
The ridges, wavy, ripple, indigo,
Hazy the desert heightening; returned
From quarantine and tested negative
Our loved one, miracle, who months ago
The airport terminal we shuttled toward
To walk alone is passenger beside me,
Who planet's safest island left to care
For us, our little one, this sickly pit
Braving again, this nation that so little
Its people serves, with virus, hunger gripped;
But now resilient earth its orbit's course
Renews, restorative the year; last week
At winter solstice watched we giants kissing,
In grand conjunction, that each other chased
The south horizon this long year along,
With gemmy brilliance and its feeble ghost

At twilight unified, above the palms
Huddled in cosmic emptiness; a prayer
We say to those we lost, their splendors found,
Dearly their names reciting, dearer still;
Of them the plague has isolated, homes
Ringing with empty silence that resound,
Or them that knotted angst unwinding can't,
Lying awake or dreamy scape-tormented
In rest ostensible, I think; this year
Reborn, may it be kinder, gentler birth,
Embracing you, all love; and we are one.

30.

This galaxy, its gaseous spiraling
And starry furnace churning hazardly
The darkly heavy density around,
Lighting, extinguishing the cosmic dust
Swirling, and there Orion's arm within,
The spur that from the spiral now emerges
More placidly, and there the unpaired sun,
Hyper aware, that sets the curvature
Of spinning rocks, bundles of liquid, gas,
And each its satellites, fields of debris—
Eccentric ice, then ringy orbitals,
The banded giant, turbulent, that heaves
If asteroid should closer drift, and there,
Sheered of its atmosphere, the ferric dirt
Enigmas positing, and just before
That swifter flutterer that center flits,
Wobbles, its toxic twin beside, the blue,
The vital earth, where, oceanic, lush
Or parching dry, the handed dominate,
Building, destroying worlds again, again,
And tenuous the layers plummeting,
The wispiness, the breathy inner sphere
With arc of firm terrain spread out below,
Billowy sea then grassy, arid ground,
The desert ridge, the boxy edifice
That on the foothill perches, there the ward
Where lady labors waiting, welcoming:
All this, before the consciousness itself
A graver framework may compose that, born,
The burdens of this planet it might bear,
They showing you, my lovely, did you see?

31.

Seated inert machines that plastic wraps
Beside, and idle implements, the hours
Counting, alone, the cranky, folded chair
My backside biter, numb, as worker, nurse
Along the hallway nurse's business work,
At times we kindly greeting, grateful me,
The pain of absence grating; mask and shield
All face, they stifling, separate all air,
Fogging the visor, sting the tender ears
The strings, and achy body, little sleep;
I'd newborn hold our baby in these arms,
But moment this I must that moment wait,
Who can't the vision of our daughter glimpse,
Not yet; and yet, my dear, I'm always there
Until such day with hands we neither hold,
Nor brace with arms; cleansing the corridor,
Its window panels through the shades imbue
With luminous fluidity all space,
The solar sequence brightening all room
As tremulous the air a heartbeat seems;
That wavy light that rains the valley long,
Where little houses ride the risen hills,
And layer of distant scrapers, blurry, peeks
Rivers of concrete sprawling there above,
And, just beneath the vanishing horizon,
The oceanic mirrors, sparking, gleam,
Kaleidoscopic hues reciprocate,
The crystal facets fragmented; those rays
The medic halls among the cactus shrubs
Pervading now our inner world they reach:
They to our eyes delighting come, or from?

And now pure spirit cradles us; each face
Is dreamer's face that dreaming faces sees,
One mind asleep that characters our script
Making us each our other's other, each,
At variance and vainly striving; now,
All love is all there is, and with all love
To earth, my dear, we warmly welcome you.

32.

Heavy the head that barely neck can lift
The bedding over, slumbering or mewling;
The flailing socks that fingers covered fall,
Recovered fall, as squirmy leggings shift,
Coldly the heat exposed, or hotly cooling,
And cries, spasmodic, urgent feeding call.

Drowsy again, the deeper slumbers flow;
What suckled was the pucker oozes drooling
And kindly hands old diapers folded haul;
True infants we unless this truth we know:
Love all.

33.

My composition this is finished now,
Complete my utterance, dear reader, you
Who author of our blessed happiness
Resplendent are, and double happiness,
Since, you without, all union dissipates,
But wording now with image this we leave:
They say the cosmic waters easeful flow
And on the surface buoyant entity
Drowses, along the languid current drifts
Snoozing, and from the navel, time to time,
The lotus blossom lifts its turgid stalk,
With color flare the folded bud unfurls
Its tender petals milk and rosy tinged,
And ring of golden stamens spiral there,
Spongy on which receptable revealed
The infant sits, whose visionary eye,
Considering each image it perceives,
Just as the bloom its fullest reaches height
Projects into the empty space surveyed
Visions of universe against the void,
And universe of universes spins,
Its peoples, things, its folded parallels
That multiply themselves past reckoning
Infinity though catching never yet;
And in each vision thinks each thing itself
A self now self directing, figment though
By infant mind contained, and vainly strives,
Existence fleeting, constancy to eke,
Though character that populates a screen;
Until each fragment perfect love recalls
That only joins, that never hurls apart,

Uniting mind, its pieces piecing whole,
Where once a bitter cell was lock and bar;
And now the many things illusive are,
We each the infant, we the flowery stem,
The sleeping body, each the river bed,
And we our lovely source; and now we say:

Our very source envelops us, its love
Sustaining, tenderly all comfort gives
And everywhere its joyful light extends,
Abstract and perfect, warmly joining us,
And everything that is, is endless love.

34. Epilogue

The vehicle the sun flood navigates;
Sounds of the radio boomingly resound,
And streets where lazily the pollen boughs
Scatter and shed along pedestrian heads,
The footfall striking, pavement stepping, air
Open and fresh, now intersection, corner
Corner and intersection crosses, turns,
The signals shifting, shifting signals, turning
The light, the car the corner intersecting,
Where autos other, constant, line the lines,
Stopping and starting, new, anew; renewed,
On glinting rubber gleams the chromy fleet,
So many minted, chassis glitterers
How proudly that display their proud display,
The rapid drivers rabidly each passing,
And older models slowly sputter, braking
Or idle idling, rusty vessels creaking,
Boxy the frames, the painting faded, pads
That squeakily restrain the motion groaning,
They holy motors all; and tapestry
Of vegetation thickly curling blurs,
To errant eyes its lushness full presents,
In which of stone the grubby mazes cleave,
And swiftly there the fray of fronds that sway
With moisture dripping from the droopy tips,
The crisper fronds discarded dry below,
Fodder for dogs that sniff and urinate;
But, look, as wind the fanning bladelet whips
The reedy surface textures bend the glare
Of day's incessant, raining luminescence
As if the fronds were shimmering itself,

The shaggy palms are shimmering itself;
And suddenly the car disintegrates,
The dash, the steering, levers, instruments
Vanish, each plastic, metal bit resolved,
Component, subcomponent, element
All atomized, my image shape retaining
Of driver driving, forward hurled in space
By void now vehicled, as if the hand
The steering held and foot the pedal tapped,
On air suspended, vacant air; the spine
In nothing nestled, that was fabric-backed,
Reclines in waves of atmospheric beaming,
And body, body launching, warmly buzzes
And through the roofless emptiness uplifts,
All level leaving, leaving form behind,
Body no longer, mere awareness moving,
To earth, its dust and thirst I goodbye giving,
Faster than thought traversing toward the lively
Contractively explosive majesties
That radiate, the life affirming sun

B. Asterism Sonnets

1.

On which to sleep, on it I thinly sleep
A mat, and droning fan beside it keep.

Not yet the bulbous lantern dimly lit
Extinguished is that scatters dimmer shade.

Belly against the floor, what well was writ
I'd read until my droopy readers fade.

My upward neck, my arching shoulders bent
The ache of day bent other way undo,

As sentence same, not knowing what is meant,
I read, rereading, reading failed renew.

Too few the hours until all loud alarm,
And nightly sky around its pole is turning.

From Thomas, sleep, do not a needed charm
Withhold, he neither room nor rest discerning.

2.

Alarm; and guttural, resounding cries,
Flailing of limbs spasmodic, weepy eyes.

A wooden crib in which our mignon sleeps,
Murky the shade the open blinds dispel.

Warmly the arm our slender creature keeps
And wipes the streamy droplets as they well.

The baby skin that baby's scent exudes
Euphoric waves releasing fumes the air.

Whole body gulping bottle-given foods,
Dribble the neck and chin the bib left bare.

Feeding, soothing our days and diaper work
Until the bright eyes brightly smiling show.

Daughter's lament would Thomas piquing perk,
And soul up from its chakra fourth would flow.

3.

Courtyard of lamps and windows lit, cement
That fissures cracking, ground unsettled, dent.

Taller the palm that upward evening touches;
The breezes whipping, flash the fronds and glow.

The hand that strains the heavy garbage clutches
And drops where, crashing lid, the odors blow.

As urban artifice against it glances,
There floats a sudden cloudlet, rosy grey.

The traffic starting stops and, stopped, advances
With engine roar the ruddy beacons stay.

Westward, Orion's belt its ancient blazes
Reveals, that pass refracted atmosphere.

Thomas watches the moon, its crescent phases,
And half suspects a ship, unseen, is near.

4.

Dazzling the day all earth and vision sears,
While rapid cars traverse what road appears.

The desert buildings, crumbling, ruined rise,
Corners by which the dusty roadway leads.

Along the plotted yard and garden flies
A sheeny feathered crow that landing feeds.

Angry the lanes where engines gusting huff,
And travel burning trash and dirt dispersed.

Pinkly, boldly against the cypress scruff
The redbuds with their wispy colors burst.

Around the parking lot we waiting snaked;
The crowded lines would slowly wander in.

Sickly and weird, his head and body ached
Once, shoulder bare, the needle stuck the skin.

5.

The waxen-leafed magnolias candent past,
Ghostly the lamps their medley pallors cast.

All day indoors while settle dust and grit
Before my bluish screen I've kept me pressed.

Now cooler gusts the courtyard squarely lit
Renew refreshing, brush the flesh undressed.

Steady it glides, the beacon bearing plane
That raucous overhead the evening rushes.

A shadow walks the grid and paved terrain
Receding now as swirling darkness hushes.

This fragrant earth exhales its garden airs,
While body stands all aching bone and sinew.

Sirius he'd watch that brightly flashing flares,
And wish this lyric art he might continue.

6.

The neighbor units vacant are again;
Is freshly painted what was shabby then.

It strikes the pavement, pad and padded toes,
Too long indoors the foot not used to walking.

Blue foxglove dangles over shrubby rose,
And grey cement is colorful with chalking.

Its fuchsia flame along the iron grating
The bougainvillea fenced and guarded sends.

Now spring is come; is gone insipid waiting,
And what the budding held the stem extends.

As hummingbirds through honeysuckle dart
Chattering, flash of brightness, flit of wing,

He shows the newborn harnessed to his heart
Each bloom its bliss, its joy each blossomed thing.

7.

It coarsens surface wide, the fallen dust
And falling gathers where I've dusted just.

Flicker the screen and keyboard activated,
The buckled desk with pen and paper spread.

By book on book the welded shelf is weighted,
Each creased or over creased or rests unread.

Coffees, they richly bitter, fragrant teas
The unit's fanned and whirling air perfume.

Dormant the table's wallet, phone and keys;
A glowing dawn will soon suffuse the room.

Morning, the vinyl blinds would turning clack,
And flinch would infant eyes the raylets strike;

Alice would laugh, our daughter laughing back,
Than which is nothing sweeter; nothing like.

8.

This arm again the venomed snake has bit,
And body wallows now that skin was split.

The voltage sparks and, ache inflaming, burns
Running the shoulder, nerves and fingertips.

Its bedding corpse confused now tossing turns
And shivers chilled when sickly fever grips.

Dizzy, the vacant room is spinning, spinning
With solace none, the frigid floor I've hugged.

What occupies this frail machine is thinning
That, disembodied, reels and staggers lugged.

Body opens the gate then stepping stumbles;
It ghostly hovers, what would step concretely.

Thomas, when all around you downward tumbles,
Hold fast! That is: release all self completely.

9.

With vertigo, I homeward bring my guest
Receiving worse whom I would welcome best.

A bloodless lethargy the limbs undoes;
Though motionless, I feel me moving still.

The shop well peopled is that vacant was,
Its foamy cups the coffees, brewing, fill.

Glass vase where peonies unfolded spring
And fragrant billow blushing petal's fluff;

Fussy and weird, I fault each little thing;
My dumber thoughts I take as finer stuff.

She lovely has her daughter grand embraced,
Today together, gone again tomorrow.

Thomas, if days you wasted, day don't waste;
This present moment joyous love; no sorrow.

10.

Across the haze and greyish hills it glooms;
Downtown, a faint, illumined specter, looms.

Both desert dry, the earth, and moldy damp,
Its buildings, dingy, lose their former sheen.

Propelled along the upward curling ramp,
Toxins emitting, speeds the quick machine.

A rusted fence that grips the gridded road
Falls loose as wind harasses plastic tents.

It trickles where robust the rivers flowed;
Cement is cracked and weedy subsidence.

The builded world collapses, grit and grime;
Its sands are glass, its ruined cities ashed.

Decay has burned your pyramids, oh time,
Your interlocking walls that eons smashed.

11.

Now spirit darling freshness kindly sends,
As foot beside the blooming myrtle tends.

Adorn the public benches, tables there
Silver and green the slender olive trees.

They dangle, strings in earthen terrace air
Of wishing notes uplifted with the breeze.

Scarlet the pomegranate branches flower
That gourdy forming swell and fuller swell.

Cascade the blossoms jacarandas shower,
And dirt is sweetly violet where they fell.

Our path by knobby pepper tree inclined
The hiving bee, the droopy cluster brings.

This labyrinth of stone the hand designed
Spiraled we step and think eternal things.

12.

At dawn, the desert buildings shiny seem;
The rays along the foggy morning beam.

The cars the crowded intersections pass
Or stop, the engine acrid gust combusting.

With pollen boughs beside the boxy glass
Cement is swirling shadow, flimsy dusting.

Gorgeous hibiscus brightly eye intrigues;
No sooner opened, shows its wilted age.

The ragged self the frantic world fatigues
With paper placard seeks its living wage.

This film in which we each appear as other,
The many others, mind has scripted same.

To you, dear reader, Thomas would be brother,
If mouth may give our perfect oneness name.

C. Sonnets to the Aten

1. Illuminations

Lucence, rapture of glass and steel, downtown,
Sleek granite shimmer-clad as light cascades;
Vast curtain walls turn mirrors base to crown
Reflecting each reflecting sheens and shades.

Burnt engines, fuming, spew obnoxious air
That wafts along stone planes and vertices;
Construction rigs send tremors, sirens blare
Through patchy groves of cypress, olive trees.

This lattice work I've walked, these parallels,
Dank tents amid the trash and putrid smells,
An arid dream that shifts but doesn't cease.

In lanes of builded luster, streets distressed
I find myself, though limping, wholly blessed
To see your lovely face and feel this peace.

2. The Cactus Garden

The desert garden years ago, now closed
In chained and padlocked fencing, skillful hands
Had wrought, the fertile flower beds had posed,
Assemblage of wood, stone and patterned sands.

Nourishing rays would bless the cactus spines,
And fleshy stalks new budding greet the breeze,
Vibrant blossoms their stems would burst and vines
To charm with nectar sweet the swarmy bees.

At watering, bright butterflies were stirred,
And swollen citrus bowed the ripened limb,
Quick perch to draw the chatty hummingbird,

As vital things exceed all bound and brim;
Unburdened minds would gather then past seeing
To dwell in stillness; deep, resplendent being.

3. A Former Life

City of sun blest temples newly built
Of stone and mud that hug the fecund shore;
The palace quays, rich current and dark silt,
Where ply by wispy reed: ship, sail and oar;

The solar disc that crimsons distant cliffs
Aligned with courtyard pylons straight arrayed;
Relief of chiseled figures, sacred glyphs
That deck each carved and painted colonnade;

All this I see, great heat and drive to build,
Visions unearthly genius shaped and willed,
Where desert bends the fertile river's brink;

And scribes he tasked to fashion hymnic phrase
To tell the things the mind can't say or think:
The boundless source, the bright, eternal rays.

4. Autumn Sonnet

The quality of light, more somber blues,
Has turning painted all things palette-matte;
The muraled walls are muted drab and flat
That flank the tents and dingy avenues.

Each bough beyond its natural habitat
Shriveling drops all leaves all drained of hues;
Too early, street lamps signal darkling views
And beam on dumpster, car, old laundromat.

At night, when vacant my dim building grows,
I restless pass through pallid haze and chill,
But neighbor windows warmth and laughter spill,

Shared mirth the private masonries enclose;
Returned, apartment empty, silent be,
But welcome stillness, peace; infinity.

5. Spiritual Dawn

Morning components: mist that glistens rose,
Empurpled gloom of shaggy palm tree shades,
Tenebrous towers loom ghostly in warm glows
That bathe decrepit streets as lamplight fades.

The waking called to work at worthless trades
Hasten to drive where traffic, slower, slows;
Along the rank, graffitied pavement grades
Shabby encampments line the lanes in rows.

They sleep in tents of crumpled tarp unrolled,
Belongings stuffed in carts and plastic bags,
And wander weathered, hungry, naked soled,

Each one my semblance, brother, self in rags.
We tattered selves that haul this harsh debris
And tread this earth: how long our penury?

6. The Passers-By

At first, we thought you body lifeless, dear,
Sprawled off the path beneath the rail and stair,
But stirring then you breathed the evening air,
Ringed by market's festive atmosphere.

Confused, you lay there writhing, toxic gear
At hand, while nurse among us meted care;
We wouldn't leave you lone or unaware
But stayed until the sirens halted, near.

Ardent desire to work annihilation
I've known, at times imagined knife or rope,
But sweet erasure, sweeter yet negation

Sustain me now past thought or speck of hope:
Inward, against this fictive self to choose,
Then, outward, gently love and joy suffuse.

7. Last Photograph

Last photograph, you have the counterpart,
As greyer gloom darkens the ocean strand
You walk where tide left wet, reflective sand,
I'm knee deep, waters turbulent, apart.

Sweet moment: smiling face I know by heart
You likewise snap my photo, phone in hand
Am I as joyful, separate though we stand
In foamy sea spray, days before we'd part?

My person, numbly working word and act
The meager car with scant possessions packed
Then drifting drove as sorrows harshly fell.

But though our minds with errant bodies mixed,
Bright constellation that burns, heavens-fixed,
You shine forever dear; dear friend, farewell.

8. Sickness and Relief

Full sickness, sudden fever claims my head
Raw sinus swelling, chills that cling to bone;
Accursed to face this swift collapse alone
I lay me, shivered body, wrapped in bed.

Might neighbor hear my enervated moan
And, knocking, offer medicine or bread?
I've scarcely strength to wonder am I dead
Or coughing croak my sorry state by phone.

Too tired to rise, fatigued to sleep, abused
I know not day or night but gaze confused,
With eyelids open, closed, on spectral things;

But sometimes hardy comfort comes new-eyed
To soothe my mind now wholly occupied
By thoughts of you: your lovely shimmerings.

9. Illuminations

Round towers and angled ones, sheer surfaces
Of limestone, marble, paneled mirror, glass;
Vast tiers and levels, verdant terraces
Fuse garden, metals, shimmering and mass.

The central building's painted pyramid
Upward emblems the sun's mosaic blazes;
Resplendent shape that pretties urban grid
As arcing day completes its daily phases.

Façade proportion shaped and music froze,
Temple to torch the sapphire, airy flows,
I'm worthy, how, to hold you, whole, in mind?

Though pattern, symbol permeate our dreams,
We tease the real that, subtle, backs all seems
With comfort of this guiding thought: be kind.

10. Wang Hsiu-Yuan

Now warmth and brilliance lend their lively rays
To streets pristine, fresh colors newly dyed;
Where courtyard fountains burble, clarified
And footfall strikes the granite-layered ways.

Bright coffee bar, your briefcase stowed beside,
To steal rich moments back from frantic days,
We meet, my loved one, joined in joyous gaze,
With nascent pangs that otherwise we'd hide.

Your picture, eyes of splendors darling, deep,
That charm me past all thought, all day I keep,
Though bent in labors, hours that blur and merge;

And heart, machine of gears and leaping flame,
As mystic chambers, heated, churn and surge,
With constant rhythm sounds your lovely name.

11. Downtown Benches

At public gardens, staggered pools reflect
Both edifice and branch as cadent breeze
Breathes on the waters, stone steps intersect
With gnarling olive, conic cypress trees.

Exhaust from noisy cars sends acrid scents
That mingle burnt with fresher, fragrant air;
The souls that slept in makeshift shelter, tents
Awake at dawn, avoid the daytime glare,

But if commercial space they breach nearby,
Guards to restrict, restrain them, nullify
Each brother ours, unbrotherly our streets;

Our fragile bodies, though they make us strange,
The mind is one with each split self it meets,
And merest love exceeds all time and range.

12. Nighttime Towers

Day's end; the ruddy sky I've missed, but work
While captures bleary eyes my bluish screen;
The twinkling hills horizon inky murk,
And haloed streets beneath show neon sheen.

The exodus of cars, each stopped machine
Now joins its pointed lamps in lines that irk;
The hungry wander ramp and bridge unseen
Seeking their nightly bed where shadows lurk.

Lighting extinguished, evening's artifice
Of countless ghostly fires and pitch abyss,
With buildings vessel-like that freeze in space,

All, blinking, beckon, flash or flare from view;
My thoughts to things that beacon every place
Now turning swoon; I feel so close to you.

13. The Shoreline Park

Gathering group, we newly ancient friends,
Where cliffs along the shoreline steeply rise,
The sandy pathway walking as it wends
All spindly palm tree, brine and brilliant skies.

At sunset stood we watching, blanket wrapped,
Crunching the pulvered quartz beneath bare feet;
The deeper crimsons, purples held us rapt
As, dimmer, dropped the orb its flare and heat.

The firmaments of stars now manifest
Their torches turned and silver planets blest,
While oceans glistened darkly, depths to shoals;

Vast omniverse of which each thing is part,
The briefest glimpse exceeds all clever art,
Shone evident that night; we grateful souls.

14. The Reading Group

You asked me why I do not speak in class,
A kindly room of cushions, light and airy;
Soft-filtered sunlight overflows much glass
To glance off trinkets, burnished statuary.

By turns, we read out loud the lilting text
Filling the space with gentle resonance,
Words that astonish, stop the mind perplexed;
Sweet music swiftly wakens mystic sense.

He said: the mustard seed is humblest grain
But sown, rich foliage graces primed terrain
To perch the birds that sprightly soar above.

Likewise, the haggard book I, seated, hold
And reading sometime see this truth unfold:
With vivid stillness bursts all perfect love.

15. The Opulent City

They round the bustling city, clouded tops
Of earthen ridges, rise and undulate,
Where patchwork desert, brush and forest copse
With splendid structure, rippling, culminate:

Secluded mansions, lawns fine-manicured
With grounds to gladden private rest and ease,
Their heavy gates and hedges full secured
From ruined streets, distressed geometries.

Grand luxuries afford what comfort, calm
For naked bodies that sleep pavement backed,
Old blankets strewn by painted brick or palm

As steady rays burn rough skin callous cracked?
Centers of wealth that gild extracted rents
And rubble leave of tarp and scraggly tents.

16. Sonnet to the Aten

Most beautiful, you rising foster life,
And dawn on rigid structures, blessings-rife,
Directing beams that scatter rosy tints
Along the lanes of murky stops and sprints.

Grimly the weary ghost that harbors strife
Receding draws unseen its flickered knife;
The hurried worker, briefcase bearing, squints
As brilliant hues refract from glass that glints.

Though body ambulate this crowded maze
Of steely concrete, breathing dust and haze,
The mind considers what must constant be;

Great warmth exceeding any bound, I'd see
All forming, formless things today, each one,
By your rays brightly, brighter than our sun.

17. Springtime Proposal

The joy of springtime's bounty lies not far
But yields itself to languor and slow walks;
Sweet jacarandas purple blooming are,
And cactus burgeons open blossom stalks.

Old neighborhood of gardens densely grown
Where eddies lift and swirl the pollen blast,
Late rays obliquely touch the townhouse stone
And brighten museum grounds we wander past.

The seasons turn, and old things new renew;
Again, the bustling block is crammed with trucks
That tenants load, unload; we're moving too,

And all is cycled change, recycled flux,
Save this: I'd have the ever-wifely guide me,
So long, my love, as you consent to bride me.

18. The Splendid Hall

Strange boulevards and figures I don't know,
Plotting the place by phone haphazard-mapped,
I'll see and huffing ocean droplets go
By stacked expanses, verticals fog-capped.

Honeyed coffee will little joy afford
My jangled nerves that nervous agitate;
Each step will draw my trepidation toward:
The splendid hall, cold corridors await.

But now, jet engines fan the runway ramped,
We file and, halting, board the cabin cramped,
Locked in our seats, our lurched ascent begin;

My armrest, as we swoop, I, rattled, clasp,
While fixed position mind would firmly grasp:
No peace, unless we deeper pass within.

19. Eventide

Our little car was rapid whirred in motion
And freely veered the ways and worn cement;
The orb behind us flamed its strange descent
As haze and fire commingled over ocean.

Dark palms adorned the city's lit extent
And faster traffic passing caused commotion;
In wordlessness aware of shared devotion
Zipping along the loop downtown we went.

The eerie buildings bent their phantom glows
Against the eastward evening's greyish rose;
We left these too and crossed, all lanes combining,

To desert hills that dwindling no light shed;
But where we go pristine our peace is shining:
Together joined, our journey's end ahead.

20. Ramana Maharshi

At times, my doubtful self most under threat,
Your ancient image I hold dearly fast;
When body breaks in shivers and cold sweat
And waves of icy dread my being blast.

When I must anxious things endure for wage
That leave all soul disjointed and askew;
When heartbeat sets against its mortal cage
To thud and thud and thud, I think on you:

Who clothed in simple cloth with rustic cane
And water kettle tread the rough terrain
Or rest cross legged, captured black and white.

Great sage, my agitations wholly cease
When your calm eyes on troubled mine alight,
Grey bearded gaze that radiates pure peace.

21. Heraclitean Fire

As if on fire the flagrant city crumbles
With masonry slow-pulverized to dust;
Its metal frames and joints, fatiguing, rust,
And steady ground itself is split and rumbles.

Surrounding hills where housing shifts and tumbles
In arid heat, their dried up mantle thrust;
Decay that smokeless makes all things combust
All ordered structure strains and heaps in jumbles.

The half-life that inherent marks all matter
Degrades all forms as forces push and shatter,
And sturdy things now turning lose their shape.

While hidden flame ensures undoings deepen,
Our love be level though the pathways steepen
That ramp us through this ruined cityscape.

22. On the Body

A human being is not a pretty thing
No matter how you dress or pamper it,
But, grown, it turns to instant festering
And must to dirt its borrowing remit.

Its healthy sinews with corruption tinged,
It withers losing strength and all strong parts,
Despite what finer venoms are syringed
What plastics are deployed, or surgeon arts.

To offer you the body is to give
A failing thing physician cannot mend;
Automaton that, striving, doesn't live
And can't its base material transcend.

Except I'm not my body, nor you yours,
And love alone our only ailment cures.

23. Night Visions

Before the deeper night my eye encumbers
I lie awake and watch the shadows shift,
While slumbrous love beside me lovely slumbers,
And cars outside their flitting lamplets lift.

My blunt fatigue with needling worry vies
Which one my weary brain might overcome;
But coaxing darkness soon gives other guise
To which my wits so close to sleep succumb.

The pitchy void seems vital luminescence
That dazzles as it evening's canvas spans
Assembling shapes to show my pupil's scans;

Then lighted mind reveals its full fluorescence,
Whole worlds arise comprising pictured things;
I'm drifting drawn in those bright patternings.

24. On Justice

At too much cost in this world justice comes
And sees blindfolded gold and paper peeking;
Its shrine requires the outlay of rich sums
For those who go redress of grievance seeking.

Practitioners that know the balance well,
Demanding that we lawful claims disclaim,
Now architects of second, harsher hell,
May make of litigation lengthy game.

Funds and accounts mean justice functions duly
To comfort them that plushly live, but me
New billings monthly posted damage newly;
Invested right yields further injury.

Except this is no world, so no one wrongs me;
An idle dream from peace too long prolongs me.

25. Airport

Again we line us, awkward animals,
For x-rays, pat-downs, as the sign assigns;
We walk misfollowing misleading signs
To reach the tumult of rank terminals.

With aching feet we line up in long lines
And crowd, too many, many urinals,
Reeking of waste and harsher chemicals,
We mass that moving to the tarmac twines.

Machine worlds gather pinching us as they,
Our guards, compel us close, too close, too near;
Controlled explosions thrust our throttled way

Packed tight in clunky planes that swerve and veer;
To travel numb in numbers closely pressed,
Bless all, my heart; and travel all ways blest.

26. On the Self

My special self what special thing will save
To make my happiness not dream but fact?
Collect how might I treasures that I crave
And fortune with my psychic will attract?

How bask in health but swollen illness stave
To keep me in advancing years intact?
How void my certain plot its certain grave
But from the natural order soul extract?

My self my doted pet I selfish keep
And cagey curb its harm and firm its joy;
And universe itself I barter cheap
To trim and deck my tricked and darling toy.

Except the self, mere concept, is not true;
Each prior self, my self thought self was too.

27. Petit Sonnet to the Aten

The radiant disc was distant, sending curled
Hibiscus leaves on layered heavens merged
With amethyst and darker lilac swirled
As current-laden lamps that flicker surged.

Rampant the city's lively murmurs verged
To evening sounds of stiller netherworld;
Earth's exhalations earthen scents expurged
And cactus shrubs their dewy buds unfurled.

The sliver Moon with silver Venus shone,
Embers to mark our nightly walker's path,
We aimless dust by desert breezes blown

To fall adrift the starlight's fragile bath.
United, then, we shared this lovely end:
My hand in yours, to all we love extend.

About the Author

Thomas Bruder has a background in ancient literature, a juris doctor, and a master's in library science.

Influences include Vergil's Eclogues and Georgics, de Vere, Goethe's Roman Elegies, Baudelaire, Rimbaud, Borges; the Hymn to the Aten, Psalm 104, A Course in Miracles; Sun Ra, Alice Coltrane, and Gilles Peterson's show on Worldwide FM.

https://thomasbruder.com

www.ingramcontent.com/pod-product-compliance
Lightning Source LLC
LaVergne TN
LVHW041340080426
835512LV00006B/551